Pioneer
Free Will Baptists
Ministers
Burial Locations
In
Alabama and
Mississippi

This book was printed in the United States of America.

To order additional copies of this book, contact:
FWB Publications
Enchanting Acres
1006 Rayme Drive
Columbus, Ohio 43207
Alton.loveless@prodigy.net
Or
www.amazon.com

FWB
FWB Publications

Introduction

Alabama and Mississippi

This book represents all that were part of the Free Will Baptist movement, consisting of the Palmer (south), Randall (north) and others such as the Stone, John-Thomas, John Wheeler Assns., NC OFWB and more.

Many of the photos are poor quality, but it was all I could find. Likewise, I do not have photos or tombstones for many of them. The information about these ministers were all that was available to me or found in archives. I made every effort to include those for which they would be remembered. Some I had no information, but research had shown they were of our denomination.

This Section is taken for a two Volume set done by this author.

Alabama

Jimmy Aldridge
Birth:
Jan. 18, 1938
Death:
Jul. 10, 2017
Burial:
Oak Hill Cemetery
Jasper
Walker County
Alabama

Jimmy Aldridge, age 79 of Jasper, passed away at his residence. Mr. Aldridge served 38 years as a missionary and Overseas Secretary for his FWB International Missions. He was much loved and esteemed by our FWB church family in the U.S. and around the world, Atta Kouakou, Africa; Nikolay Sobolev, Russia and Gerard Tynevez, France.

JJimmy Aldridge, former missionary to Côte d'Ivoire, accepted Christ as Savior at the age of 13. After graduating from Welch College in 1960, he attended Columbia Bible College for one and a half years. Appointed as missionaries in October 1962, Jimmy and his wife Janie, an R.N., departed in July of 1963 for language school. Once in Ivory Coast, they served primarily in the Bondoukou area.

Jimmy and Janie shared responsibilities in the French speaking Bible institute in Bondoukou. Jimmy worked to establish preaching points throughout the area, while Janie used her training as a registered nurse to help the many hurting people at the small medical clinic. The couple served in Ivory Coast four terms for a total of 22 years. During their stateside assignment in 1984, Jimmy was offered the newly established position of overseas secretary for the Mission. The role included counseling, advising, and troubleshooting for the various mission fields. For 15 years, the Alabama native made Nashville his home as he served in the Mission office. He retired in 1999 and returned to his home in Alabama.

Parents: Wilburn Aldridge (1902 - 1973) Hattie Thompson Aldridge (1905 - 1996)

Rev Byrd Thomas Alexander
Birth:
Dec. 10, 1913
Marion County, Alabama
Death:
Aug. 5, 1979
Pleasant Grove
Jefferson County, Alabama
Burial:
Piney Grove Free Will Baptist
Cemetery
Beaverton
Lamar County, Alabama

An ordained Free Will Baptist minister who organized Beaverton FWB church.

Brian Atwood
Birth:
June 7, 1956
Death:
March 9,, 2010
Huntsville,
Madison County, Alabama
Burial:
Maple Hill Cemetery, Huntsville,
Madison County, Alabama

For many years he was pastor of the Emmanuel FWB church in Wabash, Indiana. At the time of his passing he was pastor of the Pathway Church In Huntsville, Alabama at his untimely death.

Elder Walter Pool Bond
Birth:
May 10, 1874
Death:

Jun. 26, 1943
Burial:
Nebo Church,
Limestone County, Alabama

He Was A FWB Preacher In The
30's In Jefferson Co., Alabama.

J A Brown
Birth:
Sep. 23, 1841
Death:
Jul. 20, 1916
Burial:
Old Corinth Cemetery
Lamar County, Alabama

Early Alabama Minister in the
Vernon Association. He was
married to Lydia C Barnes Brown
(1841 - 1905) and secondly to
Francis Brown (1882 - 1906).

Tommy Lynn Burch
Birth:
Aug. 1, 1924
Death:
Dec. 13, 1996
Burial:
Weavers Cemetery, Brewton,
Escambia County, Alabama
He was an educator, minister and
builder. He was the Social
Studies professor at Free Will
Baptist Bible College. Nashville,
Tn. For 20 years. He also built
houses, churches and com-
mercial buildings in several
states.

Jackson Malone Cobb
Birth:
May 7, 1922
Alabama
Death:
Mar. 1, 1995
Fayette Co., Alabama
Burial:
Fayette Memorial Gardens
Fayette
Fayette County, Alabama

He pastored for 48 years, having been licensed in 1947, and ordained a Free Will Baptist minister in 1949. He attended FWB Bible College, Nashville, TN, from 1949-1951. His first full-time congregation was at the New Mission Church (now First FWB Church) in Fayette. His funeral was conducted at that same church 43 years later. He was a WW II Veteran, entering in 1942, fought in invasion of France and was wounded June 16, 1944. He met and married Clara Smith in 1946. He was an evangelist and had a missionary's heart, from which pastorates resulted from his own soul-winning efforts. He participated in a wide range of FWB activities, including being elected to district Home Mission boards, in both Alabama and Georgia.In the 1950's, he served as Superintendent at the FWB Childrens Home in Al. He was pastor of Union Chapel FWB Church in Crossville at the time of this death.

Charles B Craddock
Birth:
Feb. 17, 1922
Death:
May 24, 2000
Burial:
York Municipal Cemetery
York, Sumter County,
Alabama

Craddock, a native of Roper, N.C. was a pastor and minister in the Free Will Baptist Church for 26 years, serving at various churches. He served in Belk, Ala., Fulton, Miss., Ayden, N.C., Dothan, Marianna, Fla., Cottondale, Fla., and Wicksburg, Ala. He served as a Chief Petty Officer in the U.S. Coast Guard during World War II. A graduate of Free Will Baptist Bible College in Nashville, Tn., and attended Troy State University in Dothan, Alabama and Candler School of Theology in Atlanta, Georgia.

Tunis Michael Creech
Birth:
Unknown
Alabama

Feb. 22, 2002
South Carolina
Burial:
Oak Hill Cemetery,
Jasper, Walker County,
Alabama

He attended the Free Will Baptist Bible College in Nashville, Tennessee. After ordination he served as an Associate Pastor of the Fellowship Free Will Baptist Church in Flat River, Missouri, then the following Free Will Baptist churches in Thomaston, Georgia; Smithville, Mississippi; and First Free Will Baptist Church of Florence, South Carolina beginning in 1994.

Capt Benjamin F. Eddins
Birth:
Mar. 12, 1813
South Carolina, USA
Death:
Apr. 10, 1865

Tuscaloosa County
Alabama
Burial:
Greenwood Cemetery
Tuscaloosa
Tuscaloosa County
Alabama, USA

The 41st AL Infantry, under which Capt. B.F. Eddins served. He was the only Tuscaloosa native to die in Tuscaloosa County during the Civil War (1861–1865),. (Flag in AL Hist. Archives, courtesy of).

He is listed in some old church records after the war, and so is remembered here for all his service to his country and fellowman.

George Columbus Elliott
Birth:
Dec. 20, 1855
Alabama
Death:
Feb. 16, 1914
Burial:
Mount Pleasant Cemetery
Brilliant
Marion County, Alabama

Early minister in Vernon Assn. He was married to Lucinda A Elliott (1853 - 1927).

O. L. Fields
Birth:
Jan. 16, 1911
Death:
Mar. 31, 1989
Burial:
Millport City Cemetery,
Millport.
Lamar County.
Alabama

Joe Sephus Frederick
Birth:
1893
Death:
1973
Burial:
Union Hill Cemetery,
Hackleburg,
Marion County, Alabama

An ordained Free Will Baptist minister, well-loved and esteemed.

Rev John Fuller
BIRTH
1814
Walker County, Georgia, USA
DEATH
17 May 1887 (aged 72–73)
Lee County, Alabama, USA
BURIAL
Evans Cemetery
Ladonia, Russell County,
Alabama, USA

"Rev. John FULLER, was born in 1814 in Walker co. GA. His parents were Isaac and Elizabeth (EVANS) FULLER. He was ordained in 1830. He died May 17, 1887. He had been instrumental in organizing four churches, and up to the time of his death, he was active in the ministry, having at that time two churches under his care." --from "Cyclopedia of Free Baptists," published 1889, by Burgess and Ward.

"Death of Rev. John FULLER. // Rev. John FULLER, aged about 75 years, died at his home in Lee county, Ala., about seven miles west of the city, at 12 o'clock Tuesday night, after an illness of two weeks of biliousness. He leaves a wife and nine children to mourn their loss. // He was a member of the United Free Will Baptist church and had charge of several churches in that neighborhood. Rev. Mr. FULLER was a good and pure man, and all during his long life he had been a consistent Christian. // His remains were interred yesterday afternoon at 4 o'clock at Hopeful burying ground." [Columbus (GA) Enquirer-Sun newspaper, Monday, 23 MAY 1887, p. 3.]

Milton R. Gann
Birth:
Unknown
Death:
Apr. 22, 1992
Hamilton,
Marion County, Alabama,
Burial:
Poplar Log Freewill
Baptist Church Cemetery,
Hamilton,

Marion County, Alabama

A Free Will Baptist minister for 37 years, serving four churches in Alabama and Florida. He served as a denominational leader in both states being the state association moderator in Florida and moderator of the Pastors and Deacons Meeting in Alabama. A navy veteran. He did studies at Free Will Baptist Bible College.

Ellis Gore
Birth:
Oct. 3, 1800
South Carolina
Death:
Oct. 5, 1883
Pickens County, Alabama
Burial:
Gore Cemetery
Pickens County, Alabama

Ellis Gore was pastor of Mount Moriah Free Will Baptist Church from spring 1846 until September 1883, a month before his death. See Tuscaloosa News, "Church's missionary spirit still

alive after 150 years", June 5, 1996 his parents were :
Thomas Tindall Gore (1776 - 1855) and Nancy Sanders Gore (1778 - 1831) and he had two spouses: Dorcas B Gore (1804 - minutes 1866) Annie Mae Burdine Gore (1833 - 1896)

Rev Ira Derain Garrison
BIRTH
23 Apr 1873
Osborne County, Kansas, USA
DEATH
13 May 1951 (aged 78)
Winston County, Alabama, USA
BURIAL
Botush Cemetery

Haleyville, Winston County, Alabama, USA

He was an early Free Will Baptist minister that is listed the 1938 Eastern Gen. conference and is listed as one of the ministers

---

Whitaker W. Guyton
Birth:
1807
South Carolina
Death:
Feb. 4, 1860
McShan
Pickens County, Alabama
Burial:
Guyton Family
McShan
Pickens County, Alabama

Rev. Whitaker W. GUYTON, moved to AL by 1834, (date of his marriage) where he was associated with Rev. Ellis GORE, and J. Eddins, which records show when they petitioned for membership in the Baptist Union Association, Pickens Co. The Union Ass'n met in 1849, at the Mt. Moriah church which Gore had organized. By 1853 Minutes, (earliest after 1849) Mt. Moriah was no longer a part of the Association. It is reported to be the oldest Free Will Baptist church in Alabama. Rev. W. W. GUYTON, and the GORE family had kinship connections from genealogy of the families. Rev. Guyton married Luvina N (Bankhead) Nov. 29, 1834, Lamar Co. AL. Family Tree shows his parents as Abraham Guyton (1765-1816) and Martha Ellis, (1769-1838) Union Co. SC. U.S. Land records show he received 80 acres in 1839, Pickens Co, and the Alabama Homestead and Cash Entry Patents, show he received 40.015, issued May 1, 1849, from the Tuscaloosa Land Office.When the census was taken in 1860, Levina, age 48, was a widow, with Sophrona A.J. Bird, age 21, and John J. Funderburk, age 28, in HH. In the 1850 census, there was also a Mariam Bird, male, b. AL, who d. in battle in the Civil War, son of James and Mary Guyton Bird, bur. in AR, with #70799738. (Mariam and Saphrona Bird, were possibly a nephew and niece, from the m/n name given as Marion's mother.)Not much is known about the ministry of Whitaker Guyton; there is old minutes of Macedonia Primitive Bapt. church, Lamar Co. AL, which states: "Macedonia Church convened on Saturday before the 3rd Sun in July 1832. Received by letter Bro. Whitaker Guyton." Then in conference Saturday before the 3rd Sun in November 1833, "Brother Whitaker Guyton applied for a letter and obtained." This ended his membership from that church.The number of churches increased in the confines of Pickens county with Rev. Gore, and we can probably surmise, that Rev. Whitaker was involved in some of those churches after he left the Lamar Co (formerly Marion Co) AL County. His name is linked with Rev. Ellis Gore..........This burial info was posted on Pickens Co. Message Forum by "redjugwadi, on Apr. 7, 2004, showing Whitaker and Luvina's graves here, and 2 or 3 small, unmarked ones. His spouse was Luvina N Bankhead Guyton (1812 - 1887)

Jimmy Lane Harris
Birth
January 28, 1941
Blakely, Early Co., Georgia
Death
Dothan, Alabama
Buried
Gearge Cementery
Early Co., Georgia

Rev Jimmy Lane Harris, 78, passed away at the Southeast Health Medical Center in Dothan, Alabama. His funeral was held at the New Salem Free Will Baptist Church, 75 New Salem Church Road, Colquitt, GA with Rev. Mick Garner and Marty Henley officiating.

Jimmy was born on to the late Harvey Harris and Doris Lane Harris. He retired from Georgia Pacific Paper Mill after 39 1/2 years as an electrician. He has been a minister for the past 20 years and has been pastor of the New Salem Free Will Baptist Church in Colquitt, for nine years. He was a member of New Salem Free Will Baptist Church.

Daniel George Washington Hollis
Birth:
Feb. 24, 1855
Marion County,
Alabama
Death:
Feb. 4, 1930
Lamar County, Alabama
Burial:
Wofford Cemetery
Vernon
Lamar County, Alabama

Early Alabama minister. Daniel was the son of Jonathan Shelton Hollis and Barbara Milender Webb. He married Josephine Millicent "Princess Millie" Pennington, 19 Nov 1874 in Sanford Co., AL. his parents were Jonathan Shelton Hollis (1815 - 1872) and Barbara Webb Hollis (1824 - 1904). And he was married to Josephine Millicent Pennington Hollis (1851 - 1910).

Eugene Howard
Birth:
Unknown
Death:
May 9, 2011
Alabama
Burial:
Lawleys Chapel Cemetery,
Shelby County,
Alabama

Mr. Howard was saved at the age of 21. He was ordained a deacon in 1953 and to be a minister in 1957 by the Cahaba River Free Will Baptist Association. He pastored many churches all over the area. He attended school at High Point which is now Davis Chapel church in Sterrett.

He pastored Davis Chapel Church for 24 years, was assistant pastor for 3 years. Mr. Howard worked at the Stockhom Valve Fitting in Birmingham 38 years where he retired. Over the years he conducted 340 funerals, performed 213 weddings, and numerous revivals. He was a member of Ben M. Jacobs Masonic Lodge in Pell City. He served as Chaplain for many years.

Olive Free Will Baptist Church in Twin, Alabama.

William Bonnie Hughes
Birth:
Nov. 15, 1919
Death:
Nov. 16, 2004
Burial:
Fulton Bridge Cemetery
Marion County, Alabama

William Bonnie Hughes died unexpectedly on November 16, 2004, one day after his 85th birthday. Mr. Hughes answered the call to preach shortly after returning from a tour of duty in World War II and spent the next 47 years pastoring churches in Florida, Tennessee, North Carolina and Alabama. A 1953 graduate of Free Will Baptist Bible College, he served on the Colleges' Board of Trustees for more than 10 years. Mr. Hughes was instrumental in establishing youth camp programs in Tennessee and Alabama. Although retired, Hughes re-mained an active member of Mt.

Thomas Russell Hulsey
Birth:
Feb. 8, 1850
Death:
May 7, 1921
Burial:
Fairview Cemetery
Fairview
Cullman County, Alabama

Thomas married Mary Jane Mote on 16 Feb 1873 in Jefferson Co, AL. .Thomas was ordained as a Minister on 5 Jun 1884 and pastored a number of churches between 1901 and 1916 in Jackson Co AL. Churches he pastored were Pleasant Hill, Mt Tabor, Bethany, Friendship, Sulpher Springs and Center Point.

Rev Rufus Hyman
BIRTH
18 Jan 1904
DEATH
24 Oct 1964 (aged 60)
Slocomb, Geneva County,
Alabama, USA
BURIAL
Union Hill Freewill Baptist
Church Cemetery
Geneva County, Alabama, USA

Mount Olive Cemetery Waterloo
Waterloo
Lauderdale County,
Alabama
Jones Chapel Free Will Baptist Church with Bro. Danny Williams, Bro. Jack Allen Jones and Bro. Barry Kelly officiating. Mr. Jones was retired from Local #48 as a Sheet Metal worker after 20 plus years and a Minister for 52 years. He pastured 49 years in MS. and AL. and is presently pastor of Corinth Free Will Baptist Church, Waynesboro, MS.

Rev Dallas Jack Jones
Birth:
Mar. 21, 1941
Death:
Aug. 17, 2014
Burial:

W R Latham
Birth:
Nov. 10, 1830
Death:
Mar. 23, 1909
Burial:
Shiloh Cemetery
Gordo
Pickens County, Alabama
Plot: 123A

Early Alabama minister.

Rev John L Lavender
BIRTH
26 Jun 1911
DEATH
18 Apr 2005 (aged 93)
BURIAL
Shiloh Cemetery
Gordo, Pickens County,
Alabama
PLOT   134A

Woodrow Matthews
Birth:
Mar. 4, 1919
Death:
Mar. 2, 2012
Burial:
Guin City Cemetery,
Guin,
Marion County, Alabama

Woodrow Matthews, age 92, of Guin, Alabama passed away at the Northwest Regional Medical Center in Winfield, Alabama. Born in Mine LaMotte, Missouri. He was united in marriage to Blanche Huffman on October 28, 1939. Matthews answered the call to preach in 1939 and was ordained in 1940. He pastored churches in Missouri and Oklahoma. In 1973, he moved to Guin, Alabama and pastored the Mt. Olive FWB Church until 1985. He then accepted the pastorate of Barnesville FWB Church in Hamilton, Alabama. In 1998 after 58 years of faithful service.

Bro. Matthews was actively involved in the Missouri FWB State Association, serving on the state youth camp board for many years, the state general board, and moderator of the Missouri State FWB Association.

As pastor of the Mt. Olive FWB Church, he was involved in the development of the Trinity Youth Camp, and served on the camp board for a number of years. He also served as moderator of the State Pastor and Workers Conference. Bro. Matthews was an active supporter of state and national programs, and especially missions. Numerous pastors, pastors' wives, home and foreign missionaries have come from his churches throughout his years of ministry. His philosophy of ministry was: "If you genuinely love your people, your people will love you."

Trellis L Mayhall

Birth:
Aug. 13, 1933
Death:
Jan. 29, 1998
Burial:
Winston Memorial Cemetery, Haleyville, Winston County, Alabama

He was ordained to preach in 1964 as a Free Will Baptist minister. He served churches in Florida, Georgia, Indiana and Alabama.

Three men answered the call to preach during his pastorate at the Free Water Free Will Baptist Church in Alabama.
He was active in denominational work serving as moderator of Alabama's Jasper Association, Executive Board Member, General Board Member, and Ordaining Council Member.
He graduated from the Alabama Bible Institute.

Elihue Roy Mayo

Birth:
Sep. 13, 1923
Boyd County, Kentucky
Death:
Sep. 17, 2011
Alabama
Burial:
New Home Cemetery, Coffee County, Alabama

He was one of our WW II heroes, serving in the Army Aircorp. He received a purple heart, three bronze stars and many medals during his service and tour over Normandy during D-day. He was an ordained minister and had pastored churches in Gadsden, Wattsville, Pell City, Adamsville, Enterprise, Alabama and Houston, Texas. He served as a Home Missionary from 1973 to 1992.

Rev Peter McGee, Jr

Birth:
1825
Tuscaloosa
Tuscaloosa County, Alabama
Death:
Apr. 7, 1887
Vernon
Lamar County, Alabama
Burial:
Walnut Grove Cemetery
Vernon
Lamar County, Alabama

An early Free Will Baptist ordained minister, who was well loved and esteemed.

W H McGee
Birth:
1843
Death:
unknown
Burial:
Hargrove Cemetery
Gordo
Pickens County, Alabama

A member of the Mt Moriah Association.

Rev. Rodger William Milling Sr.
BIRTH
July 01, 1940
Piedmont, AL
DEATH
March 10, 2020
St. Francis Hospital,

Columbus, GA
Burial:
Lakeview Memory Gardens
Phenix City, AL

Funeral services were in the Chapel of Vance Brooks Funeral Home, Phenix City, AL with his sons, Rev. David Milling and Rev. Mark Milling officiating. Committal services were held at Lakeview Memory Gardens with the Rev. Alan Griffith officiating.

Rev. Milling was born son of the late David Leon Milling and Vera Evelyn Sieber Milling. He was a former Drum Major for Central High School, a member of Central Baptist Church and had retired from the State of GA as the Maintenance Supervisor for the Jack T. Rutledge Correctional Center. Rev. Milling served as Pastor at Bethel Free Will Baptist Church and White Rock Free Will Baptist Church and ministered in several other churches as needed. Rev. Milling served as a Trustee for the Free Will Baptist Children's Home in Eldridge, AL for over 20 years. He was an avid Alabama Football fan, enjoying the games with family and friends as often as possible.

Herman A. O'Donnell
Birth:
May 20, 1896
Death:
Nov. 12, 1985
Burial:
Mount Zion Methodist Church
Cemetery,
Ragland,
St. Clair County,
Alabama

Luther D Nance
Birth:
Jul. 19, 1920
Death:
Dec. 9, 1993
Burial:
Cullman City Cemetery,
Cullman,
Cullman, County, Alabama

He was an ordained Free Will Baptist minister, pastor, and was in the early minutes of the Nat'l Ass'n of FWB, serving on the FWB League Board in 1945 to? He was living and pastoring in Detroit, MI at the time.

Ottis Ray Parmer
Birth:
unknown
Death:
Jan. 24, 2015
Burial:
West Alabama Memorial ardens
Gu-Win, Marion County,Alabama

Ottis Parmer died. Published in The Birmingham News from Jan. 24 to Jan. 25, 2015

Rev John T Quick
Birth:
Mar. 14, 1901
Death:
Apr. 3, 1964
Burial:

Laodicea Freewill Baptist
Church Cemetery
Hanceville
Cullman County, Alabama

An ordained Free Will Baptist
minister/leader whose name
appeared with others in 1930
Minutes, as 'making a great
impact' in the church, state and
nation, in 1929-30.

J R Robertson
Birth:
Apr. 22, 1839
Death:
Nov. 29, 1912
Burial:
Shiloh Methodist Episcopal
Church Cemetery
Hightogy
Lamar County, Alabama

Minister in the Mt. Moriah
Association.

Rev Angus L. Sellers
BIRTH
28 Dec 1854
Pine Level, Montgomery County,
Alabama, USA
DEATH
6 Jan 1937 (aged 82)
Crenshaw County, Alabama, USA
BURIAL
Rocky Mount Cemetery
Highland Home, Crenshaw
County, Alabama, USA
PLOT   Section 4

He was a registered Free Will
Baptist minister from Georgia at
the 1936 session of the Eastern
conference   meeting   in
Glennville, Georgia.

Thomas M. Scott
Birth:
May 10, 1931
Pike County
Alabama
Death:
May 18, 2014
Red Bay
Franklin County
Alabama
Burial:
Kimbro Cemetery
Dozier, Crenshaw County
Alabama

He was a member of Red Bay Free Will Baptist Church where he was a former pastor for 15 years. He was a veteran of the U.S. Air Force serving 20 years. Services were held at the Red Bay Free Will Baptist Church with Bro. Steve Lindsay, Bro. Barry Raper, David Corum and Ron Scott officiating. Services was held at First Baptist Church, Dozier, Al.

Rev Thomas Alden Springfield
Birth:
May 1, 1881
Death:
Jan. 16, 1972
Burial:
Shiloh Cemetery,
Gordo
Pickens County,
Alabama
Plot: 30A

Minister.

Thomas Woods Springfield
Birth:
Mar. 11, 1854
Lamar County, Alabama
Death:
Aug. 25, 1922
Ethelsville, Pickens County,
Alabama.
Burial:
Ethelsville Cemetery
Ethelsville
Pickens County, Alabama
He was an early minister that joined with Ellis Gore in the work in Alabama after which the

churches multiplied in the countries throughout the region making it necessary to divide the Mt. Moriah Association.. He served 46 years. Springfield was the son of Thomas Springfield and Emily Woods. He married Amanda Catherine Guin on 10/10/1875 in Sanford County, Alabama.

William James Springfield
Birth:
Sep. 15, 1852
Death:
Jul. 6, 1883
Burial:
Vernon Cemetery, Vernon Lamar County, Alabama
Early minister in Alabama. He was the son of Emily Calloway Woods and Thomas Walker Springfield, and was married to Tessie M Haley (1858 - 1891).

Julius. J. Staab
Birth:
Apr. 14, 1906
Alabama
Death:
Apr. 22, 1983
Alabama
Burial:
Forest Crest Cemetery, Birmingham, Jefferson Co., Alabama

He was an officer in the Alabama State Assn. serving as Assistant Moderator

J. D. Stephens
Birth:
Feb. 21, 1826
Death:
Apr. 24, 1896
Burial:
Deerman Chapel Cemetery Steele
St. Clair County, Alabama

Early FWB minister in Alabama.

Rev Michael E. Vail
Birth:
Nov. 5, 1822
Lancaster County
South Carolina
Death:
Jul. 24, 1900
Lamar County, Alabama
Burial:
Mount Pleasant Cemetery
Lamar County, Alabama

Michael E. (Mikel) Vail was the son of Jeremiah Vail and Mary Funderburk. He was a nephew of Jeremiah Vail b. 1817, who came to Bienville Parish, Louisiana, in 1859 from Pickens Co., Alabama. Found his name in early FWBapt church records, as ministers serving the Mt. Moriah Association in 1851. Alabama CSA veteran.

Leon D. Vance
Birth:
1937
Death:
1994
Burial:
New Horizon Memorial Gardens,
Dora, Jefferson County,
Alabama

Mississippi

Matthew Ranson Allen
Birth:
Oct. 5, 1888
North Carolina
Death:

Jul. 21, 1953
Mississippi,
Burial:
Sherman Cemetery
Sherman
Pontotoc County, Mississippi

Minister, teacher; who pastored churches in Monroe Co. MS. His name is listed in book by Rev. G. C. Lee, Sr., in 1949. College educated he taught school after college. As a minister of the gospel it was said that he served the Lord in pastoring several churches in N. E. MS including Pearce's Chapel in Monroe County near Smithville, MS. Allen married Lillian L. Brasfield, 19 Dec 1914. Born to that union included sons: Doyle, Thomas, an Eustace Dorsey Allen.

Rev James Earl Cosby
Birth:
Jul. 29, 1947
Canton
Madison County
Mississippi
Death:
Mar. 1, 2015
Ashland

Ashland County
Ohio
Burial: Andrews Chapel
Cemetery
Kearney Park
Madison County
Mississippi

Rev. James Earl COSBY, 67, was born Elex and Beulah (Allen) Cosby in Canton, Mississippi and had lived in Mansfield, Ohio the past 47 years. James was employed in the steel industry first with DSL where he served as the first African American Union President of Steelworkers Local Union #7597 serving for 20 years, and retiring from Empire Detroit Steel Mill in 2004 after 21 years of service.

James became an ordained minister in 1993 and pastored several churches in the Mansfield and Willard, Ohio area. In his ministry Rev. Cosby continued to break barriers by being the first African American to either join or pastor in the following conferences and churches: joined and ordained through the Ohio Northern Conference Free Will Baptist, pastored the Free Will Baptist Church in Clyde, current pastor of Paradise Free Will Baptist Church in Mansfield, and joined the Lorain-Cuyahoga Conference Free Will Baptist. Rev. Cosby was very involved in his community, and church as a member of the Mansfield Interdenominational Ministerial Alliance where he was former vice president, NAACP where he held numerous positions, Richland County Democratic Party, founder of the Cosby Educational Heritage Center located in the Ocie Hill Building. His accomplishments were many and too numerous to name them all.

Joyce Layfette Gore
Birth:
December 2, 1932
Death:
December 26, 2018
Hurley, Mississippi
Burial:
Corinth Free Will Baptist Church
Cemetery
Wayne County, MS

Bro. Gore spent his life in ministry with Mississippi Free Will Baptist Churches. He pastored for over 60 years and started several churches through Mississippi Home Missions of Free will Baptist. He was always willing to preach or sing about his love for Jesus and praised Him with his voice and his life.

The funeral service was held Corinth Free Will Baptist Church with Bro. Gerald Gann and Bro. Malcolm Garrett officiating.

William Fondren
Birth:
Dec., 1855
Alabama
Death:

Mississippi
Burial:
Gauley Cemetery, Pittsboro, Calhoun County, Mississippi

He came to Mississippi sometime between 1870 and 1880, where records show him as performing a number of marriages. He was a

Free Will Baptist minister, but it is unknown where and when he was ordained.

Luther D. Gibson
Birth:
Aug. 20, 1920
Mississippi
Death:
May 2, 1992

Booneville,
Prentiss County, Mississippi
Burial:
Tuscumbia Baptist,
Old Hwy 145, Booneville,
Prentiss County, Mississippi

Jesse Heath was 22 years old when he and four of his brothers served with Stanford's battery at Shiloh. Here, he poses years after the war with his wife, Sally Little, who became the oldest living person in Mississippi in the 1930s when she reached the age of 102.

A well-known Free Will Baptist pastor and denominational leader. He pastored for 49 years in Mississippi except for 5 years in Missouri. As a leader, he was the moderator of two district associations and for 25 years served on the Board of Trustees of the Free Will Baptist Bible College in Nashville Tennessee. *The Lumen*, the college yearbook, was dedicated to him in 1976. A Navy veteran serving in World War II. He was a pastor's pastor and a role model for many. He held a Bachelor of Arts degree from Free Will Baptist Bible College and did graduate study at Columbia Bible College in Columbia, South Carolina.

Jesse Heath
Birth:
Unknown
Death:
Unknown
Inscription:
Burial:
Calvary Cemetery
Carroll County, Mississippi
Plot: Unknown Dates Stanfords
BatteryMiss E Arty. CSA

M. L. Hollis, Sr.
Birth:
Sep. 1, 1898
Death:
Feb. 18, 1974
Amory, Mississippi
Burial:
Masonic Cemetery
Amory, Monroe County,
Mississippi

The 17 year old saw mill worker had only completed eight years of school, but God had called him to preach and for several years he fought that calling. Mr. Hollis was licensed to preach in June, 1918. He began holding services and revivals, but somehow he just couldn't shake the conviction that God wanted him to finish school. He tried several ways to get the money to further his education, but each time the door was closed. Finally, Damascus Free Will Baptist Church near Meridian, Mississippi asked Brother Hollis to come to their church for a revival. Meridian seemed to be very far from his home in Vernon, Alabama, yet, he realized this was a call from the Lord. He soon found himself standing on the train depot in Meridian waiting to be met by two men from the church. However, these two men mistook him for a young boy and they left without the evangelist! Brother Hollis finally managed to get to the church - just in time for the service. As he walked to the pulpit, an elderly man with a beard stroking his belt, said in tones loud enough for that frightened 17-year-old to hear, "If that is our chance for a preacher, we are out!" But God hadn't struck out. At the close of the revival the church offered to call the teenage preacher as pastor of the church and pay his expenses while he finished school. So, Mr. Hollis started back to school in the ninth grade. He finished high school graduating second in his class. The Damascus Church then sent Brother Hollis to Beason Jr. College in Meridian for two years. Several years later, in 1927, Brother Hollis received a scholarship from the John D.Rockefeller Foundation to attend Vanderbilt School of Religion in Nashville, Tennessee. He attended six weeks a year for four years. He later went to Moody Bible Institute in Chicago, Illinois. After God had called and prepared His vessel, He began to open doors of service. In 1927 he went to a full time church in Bryan, Texas. He then returned to Red church Bay, Alabama in

1929, where he served as it's pastor for 21 years. Following his five year ministry at the Damascus church, Mr. Hollis accepted the pastorate of five country churches in Alabama for four years. However, during these churches he was already serving, he also had the times the newly organized churches had the responsibility of simultaneously having services on Saturday night or Sunday ministering in five to eleven other mornings at nine o'clock, or Sunday churches, preaching five to six sermons in the afternoon to enable Brother Hollis to pastor or preach every weekend. This schedule was maintained as a typical story repeated 24 times during these years of his ministry Brother Hollis organized many Free Will Baptist churches. As far as is known there were no Free Will Baptist known who organized more churches as he did. He began as a Free Will Baptist minister in extensive evangelistic endeavors and organizing churches. Because of his ability and dedication, he was elected chairman of the National Home Missions Board in 1938. Not only is Mr. Hollis known for his pastoral and organizational work. but he has been one of the most widely used evangelists in 20th century in Free Will Baptist history. Whether the revival was held in brush-arbors, tents, churches, or auditoriums, God blessed the revival work of M. L. Hollis. One of the best remembered revivals in this evangelist's ministry was held at Pearce Chapel Free Will Baptist Church in Smithville, Mississippi. At the close of the week 78 converts were baptized. Because of the large number of baptismal candidates several hundred people gathered at the river to watch. Many doubted that the short evangelist could accomplish the strenuous task by himself. However, he not only baptized all 78, but he did ¡t ¡n exactly 32 minutes! Manv called Mr. Hollis again and again as evangelist. The Damascus Church where he first pastored has had him in revival 33 times. Brother Hollis' ministry spanned over 55 years with his longest pastoral tenure being 35 years at the Pearce Chapel Church. During these years he had become well-known for his prophetic messages. One of the highlights of his ministry was his visit to he Holy Land. Even though in his 70s he thrilled to see the area where many Biblical prophecies, of which he has so long preached, will be fulfilled. It is impossible to fully realize what this veteran preacher has meant to the Lord's work. A numerical summary of his work is given in his own words: "l have organized 24 churches, held revivals in 23 states, baptized more than 6,000 converts, received into Free Will Baptist churches over 10,000 members, and married numerous couples and average over 100 funeral a year. His spousd were Effie Mae Hollis

(1898 - 1969) who married in 1922 and Helen Streety who he married have the death of Effie..

Inscription:
A Devoted Husband, A Loving Father. And A Faithful Soldier Of The Cross Of Jesus Christ

James H. Norwood
Birth:
Apr. 26,1866
Death:
Nov. 29,1940
Mississippi
Burial:
Antioch Cem.,
Toccopola
Pontotoc Co. MS

Parents were Washington Pinkney Laben NORWOOD, and Mary (Farrar) NORWOOD.

He married Margaret "Maggie" (Carr) NORWOOD, 4 Mar 1886 in Pontotoc Co., MS.

He was an ordained Free Will Baptist minister, who worked in several localities in northeastern Mississippi, including counties, Calhoun, Kemper, Lee, Lafayette and Pontotoc, as well as Hood Co. TX in 1900, and Atascosa Co., TX in 1910.

His name is listed with the old pioneer ministers in these Mississippi areas before 1900 and afterward, who went many times without any remuneration for their services. He established the Stetson's Chapel church before 1909, in Lafayette Co. and he pastored throughout the area, as well as doing the work of of an evangelist with great success in his meetings. A friend, Rev. G.C. Lee, Sr., wrote of him, "...he was a mighty power in the ministry of the gospel of the Lord." He was always ready to help another minister whenever he could, but was loyal to his church.

He was beloved and esteemed by the many friends and minister brethren he worked with.

Daniel Wyatt Jones, Jr
Birth:
Mar. 23, 1930
Death:
Apr. 20, 2011
Burial:
Little Brown Cemetery,
New Site,
Prentiss County, Mississippi
He was a member of New Lebanon Freewill Baptist

Church, a retired Freewill Baptist preacher and a sheet metal mechanic. He was the son of Rev. D.W. Jones Sr.

Rev Norlin Dencil Jones, Sr
Birth:
Feb. 3, 1928
Death:
Mar. 16, 2003
Burial:
Jones Chapel Cemetery
Prentiss County
Mississippi
Plot: Section behind the church

A Free Will Baptist minister, he pastored the Randall Memorial and First Free Will Baptist Churches in Memphis from 1955 to 1966. He served as home missionary/church planter for the State of Tennessee and the National Association of Free Will Baptists. He founded the First Free Will Baptist Church of Jackson, Tenn. He then moved to Daytona Beach, Fla., where he founded the Daytona Beach Free Will Baptist Church. He also pastored several Free Will Baptist Churches in Mississippi.

He served in the U.S. Army from 1946-1948 and was stationed in Tokyo, Japan. After his marriage he moved to Memphis and worked as a tool and die pattern maker for International Harvester Corp. until entering the ministry full time.

Services with the Rev. Terry Booker and the Rev. Leonard Ball officiating. WW II U.S. Army Veteran.

John A. Killingsworth
Birth:
Dec. 5, 1852
Mississippi
Death:
Jan. 4, 1925
Calhoun County, Mississippi
Burial: Pittsboro Cemetery,
Pittsboro,
Calhoun County, Mississippi

A Free Will Baptist pioneer minister/pastor in Mississippi.

George Cullen Lee
Birth:
May 3, 1887
Calhoun County, Mississippi

Death:
Jul. 12, 1971
Calhoun County, Mississippi
Burial:
New Gauley Cemetery,
Calhoun City,
Calhoun County, Mississippi

A Mississippi FWB minister for over 62 year and a man of faith. From the Calhoun newspaper, "Rev Lee was one of Calhoun County's best citizens and in addition, is a forceful, eloquent and successful preacher. If we were called on to name most valuable citizen of Calhoun City, Rev. Lee would be among those who would come to our mind. He lives his religion every day of his life; he meddles with no person's affairs, but is ever ready to help and advise when there is trouble or sorrow. He is not the spectacular, egotistical type of preacher--he goes about his work quietly, confidently, full of high purpose. George Lee is a product of Calhoun and we are proud of him." He was called to preach in his home church of Gauley Free Will Baptist Church west of Calhoun City, MS and pastored there from 1909 until the late 60's or approximately 60 years. He married Estelle Whitworth in 1909 and they had 8 children. Clara Mae, who died in infancy, Marie, Lillian, Lora, Nellie Helen, Wanda and G.C., Jr. followed.

He pastored country churches in Mississippi during his ministry and a partial listing of them were: New Gauley, New Life,

Priceville, Antioch, Bethlehem, Lee's Chapel, Stetson's Chapel, Beech Springs, McGregor's Chapel Springdale. Those are some of the ones I recall going to with him but this is an incomplete list. (GC Lee,Jr.)

He married hundreds of couples and conducted at least 500 funerals.

Rev George Pardon Mayo
Birth:
Jun. 27, 1875
Tishomingo
Tishomingo County
, Mississippi
Death:
Oct. 12, 1957
Booneville
Prentiss County,
Mississippi
Burial:
Little Brown Cemetery
New Site
Prentiss County,
Mississippi

Mississippi Free Will Baptist minister, who served as assistant moderator in 1923, and name appears in minutes of Northeast Mississippi Association.

William Garland Prude
Birth:
Nov. 22, 1895
Death:
Jun. 12, 1966
Burial:
Tupelo Memorial
Park Cemetery

Tupelo
Lee County,
Mississippi
Plot: Section C - Row 19

Iris Lyndon Stanley
Birth:
Mar. 19, 1906
Saltillo, Lee County, Mississippi
Death:
Sep. 27, 1993
Saltillo, Lee County, Mississippi
Burial:
Spring Hill Cemetery,
Saltillo,
Lee County, Mississippi

He was the first Superintendent of the Free Will Baptist Home for Children in Greenville, Tennessee. He served in this position for 25 years. He started the Harris Memorial Free Will Baptist Church in Greenville so the children would have a Free Will Baptist church to attend.

He was a World War II veteran of the U.S. Army and a former

schoolteacher with the Lee County school system. He was a well-known music director assisting the late Rev. H. L. Hollis in starting many Free Will Baptist churches in Mississippi and Alabama.

He was frequently used as the song leader of the National Association at its annual sessions.

George W. Wages
Birth:
May 5, 1886
Death:
Jun. 27, 1972
Burial:
Blue Mountain Cemetery
Blue Mountain
Tippah County, Mississippi

Rev. Geo. Washington Wages was a FWB minister, mentioned in a book pub. in 1949, by Rev. G.C. Lee, Sr., who had association with him. In the 1940 census he states his occupation. as 'minister.' He was esteemed by those who knew him. George W. Wages married Viola Sewell on September 15, 1907. They had 6 children.

To Call His Soul To The Life Immortal Where Souls A-Weary Shall Rest With God.

Randy Wright
Birth:
Aug. 13, 1960
Amory
Monroe County
Mississippi
Death:
Feb. 7, 2015
Fayette
Fayette County, Alabama
Burial:
Masonic Cemetery
Amory
Monroe County, Mississippi

Bro. Randy Wright, 54, of Guin, Ala., passed away in Fayette Medical Center in Fayette, Ala.

He is the son of Henry Grady Wright and the late Mary Mildred Schumpert Wright. He was pastor of Piney Grove Free Will Baptist Church for the past 25 years. He was Chairman of the Home Mission Board and had served on the Trinity Youth Camp Board and ALCAP Board. He was a former Chairman of the Acts 1:8 Committee, and he served 11 years as Chaplin of Hospice of Northwest Alabama. He loved music, was a trumpet player, and had also been a DJ since he was 15 years old.

Services were at the Guin First Baptist Church with Bro. Mickey Crane, Bro. Rick Cash, Bro. Danny Williams, Bro. David Crowe and Bro. Jack Whitley officiating.

www.ingramcontent.com/pod-product-compliance
Lightning Source LLC
Chambersburg PA
CBHW071319280526
45788CB00004B/1946